To Fred Fox

Progressive Studies for Trumpet

and other treble clef brass instruments

John Miller

© 1993 by Faber Music Ltd
First published in 1993 by Faber Music Ltd
3 Queen Square London WC1N 3AU
Music processed by Silverfen Ltd
Cover illustration by Debbie Hinks
Cover design by M & S Tucker
Printed in England by Caligraving Ltd

ISBN 0-571-51320-4

To buy Faber Music publications or to find out about the full range of titles available
please contact your local music retailer or Faber Music sales enquiries:

Faber Music Ltd, Burnt Mill, Elizabeth Way, Harlow, CM20 2HX England
Tel: +44 (0)1279 82 89 82   Fax: +44 (0)1279 82 89 83
sales@fabermusic.com   www.fabermusic.com

FABER *ff* MUSIC

Preface

Progressive Studies for Trumpet continues the didactic thread established in **Simple Studies for Beginner Brass**, aiming to develop technique in tandem with musicianship. The studies are arranged so as to provide progressively increasing challenges throughout the book, from grade 4 (AB) level upwards.

As in **Simple Studies**, indications of style are given throughout, and some descriptive titles offer further pointers. *Optimum* tempi are given and should be regarded as eventual goals rather than mandatory instructions. Technical suggestions and occasional listening recommendations are also provided. The student should be encouraged to transpose the studies liberally, in order to build range, stamina and other skills.

Although these studies have been devised principally for the trumpet they may obviously be used by all treble clef brass instruments, though not all will be suitable for trombone, and french horn players may wish to adapt and extend the lower register of some studies.

John Miller

JOHN MILLER is one of Britain's leading brass teachers. He read music at King's College, Cambridge, and subsequently studied trumpet in USA. He freelanced extensively in London, notably with the London Sinfonietta and the Philip Jones Brass Ensemble, and was a member of the Philharmonia Orchestra between 1977 and 1994. He is a founder member of the Wallace Collection.

He has been a professor of trumpet at the Guildhall School of Music and Drama, London, since 1979, a brass tutor of the National Youth Orchestra of Great Britain since 1991, and in 1993 was elected a Fellow of the Guildhall School. His teaching activities to date have included masterclasses in China, Finland, Germany, Japan, USA and the Paris Conservatoire.

Contents

1. Bothie Ballad

Sweet and smooth ♩=90 or less

Phrasing and sound quality are the fundamentals of fine playing. Therefore in this ballad aim to extend your breath control by breathing in eight bar phrases as indicated.

2. The Upward Slur

Smoothly ♩=84

Slurring up is harder than slurring down. To slur up, co-ordinate use of the stomach muscles (to support the air column) with embouchure and correct tongue position. Simply think *taa-ee-ee* through each three-note ascending figure, keeping an open feeling in the throat. I have given one uniform dynamic – so aim for complete smoothness.

4

3. Mexican Sunset

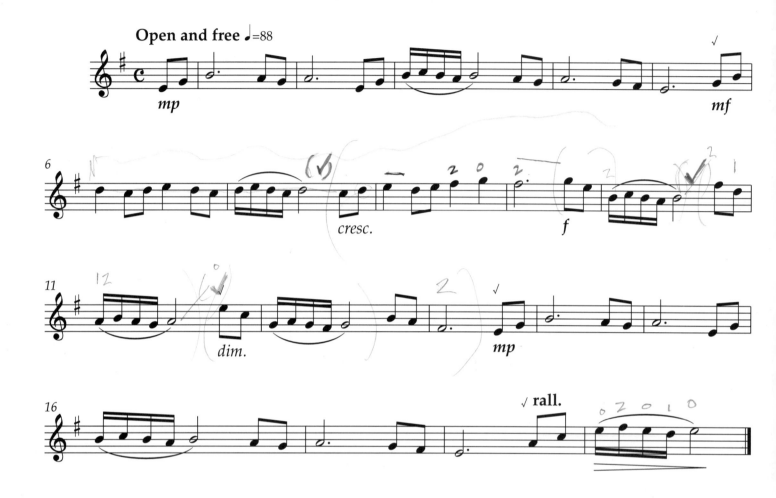

Here I have suggested extended phrases, so again see if you can manage these without sacrificing smoothness! This is a perfect opportunity to develop fine sound quality. Always remember, the higher the pitch, the more support is required. Therefore keep the stomach firm in the last bar, and retain open sound and true pitch.

Going Solo · Trumpet

first performance pieces for trumpet/cornet in B♭ with piano

erste Vortragsstücke für Trompete/Kornett in B und Klavier
premières pièces de concert pour trompette ou cornet en si bémol et piano

John Miller & Leslie Pearson

© 1993 by Faber Music Ltd
First published in 1993 by Faber Music Ltd
3 Queen Square London WC1N 3AU
Cover illustration by John Levers
Cover design by M & S Tucker
Printed in England
All rights reserved

FABER *ff* MUSIC

1. All in a Garden Green

Traditional
arr. John Miller

2. Steal Away

Spiritual
arr. John Miller

3. Bulgarian Dance

Bulgarischer Tanz   Danse de Bulgarie

John Miller

4. British Grenadiers

Traditional
arr. Leslie Pearson

5. The Albatross

Der Albatros *L'Albatros*

John Miller

6. Fairest Isle

Henry Purcell
arr. Leslie Pearson

7. John come kiss me now

William Byrd
arr. John Miller

8. Tongue in Cheek

Zum Schmunzeln   Pour délier les langues

Leslie Pearson

9. Greensleeves

Anon.
arr. John Miller

11/12/96

Freely ♩. = c. 60

10. Mexican Sunset

Sonnenuntergang in Mexiko   Coucher de Soleil Mexicain

John Miller

11. Habanera

Georges Bizet
arr. John Miller

12. Ich ruf' zu Dir

I pray to you   Reçois ma priére

J.S. Bach
arr. Leslie Pearson

13. The Hump

Der Buckel   La Bosse

John Miller

14. Jesu, Joy of Man's Desiring

Jesus meine Zuversicht   Jésus que ma joie demeure

J.S. Bach
arr. Leslie Pearson

15. Sunset Strip

Leslie Pearson

* small notes optional

4. Articulation

To achieve clean articulation, don't forget to keep the stomach muscle support firm, as this helps to keep the throat (and consequently the sound) open. Articulation then has a good foundation, and the tongue can act as a valve cleanly behind the upper teeth. Think phonetically: *too too too too too—*

5. Prairie Song

The three American composers Gershwin, Copland and Bernstein all treated the trumpet, at times, as a sweet solo instrument. Aim to cultivate a wide open feel of sound and phrasing. I suggest listening to Copland's *Quiet City*, or Gershwin's *An American in Paris*.

6. March

In this burlesque march provide character by playing the rhythm of bars 1 & 2 precisely, but slightly "spreading" bars 3, 4, 8 (especially the triplets) and 14 to 17. This style is similar to some of the orchestral writing of Shostakovich and Prokofiev.

7. Fifths

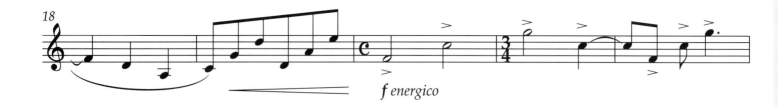

Here, correct support of the air will hold the pitch of such notes as the G in bar two. Otherwise the higher notes will be pinched in quality and sharp. Cultivate a sweet *cantabile* in bars 10-19.

8. The Octave Leap

Using the same fundamentals as in *The Upward Slur* – especially the use of abdominal muscles, embouchure and tongue (*ta-tee*, *ta-teeeeee*) – practise this piece slowly and cleanly, until you achieve accuracy with equal timbre, before speeding up! Advanced players may transpose this study as for trumpet in E♭ – up a fourth.

9. The Third Slide

The notes at the foot of the stave, D and Db, need flattening by pushing the mobile third slide by (respectively) about 1 cm and 2 cm. Great care will be needed in bars 13, 15 and 17 to keep true fifths between Ab and Db! The simple dynamic mark and the many tenuto indications are to encourage you to aim for complete evenness – with no bulges!

10. The Dynamic Duo

Production practice, both loud and soft, is a good cure for hesitant attack. When playing *forte* really let go of the air, keeping an open throat, and when playing *piano* try to keep the air well-supported, but the inner embouchure pliant, to produce a smooth and controlled sound. **Rest well** after this exercise, for if played properly it demands much concentration and stamina.

12

11. Stealthy living

A controlled and centred tone in the low register requires a firm but open embouchure. Think phonetically of *toe* or *taw* rather than the *taa* of the middle register, or the higher set *tee*. Descending scales concentrating on equal quality and centring can be a good preparation. Don't blow too hard when playing *piano* in the low register – aim for sufficient air at low velocity.

12. Rubber lips

Progress in lip flexibility is best gained in a controlled manner. Therefore try isolating short passages, such as bar 2, and practising with a metronome well under tempo until you achieve flexibility with absolute rhythmic precision. Then increase the speed. Listen to Britten's *Fanfare for St Edmundsbury* for three trumpets, or *Serenade* for tenor, horn and strings.

13. Morning

Take care to differentiate between semiquaver and quaver upbeats. When playing *piano legato* be firm with both the fingers and with support, even though not using much air!

14. Major Crabwise

Fluency in major scales is of paramount importance in playing any instrument, and this exercise condenses practice greatly. Note that transposition of the study of up to a fourth or a fifth will thoroughly cover the normal range! Start slowly and build up consistency, speed, dexterity and strength. Double tongueing may be utilised, and various alternatives may be applied **throughout**, such as the examples of dynamics shown (e.g. bars 15ff etc.), and the three rhythmic patterns, A (bar 22), B (bar 23) and C (bar 24).

15. The Trill

Trills which cross the harmonic series, such as in bars 5-8 and 17-20, are trickier than those that don't. Therefore isolate and practise slowly those that stick. It is also valuable to investigate alternative fingerings, such as the upper E-F trill in bars 29 and 32, played $\frac{1}{2}$-1.

16. Major and Minor Seconds

A delicate touch and high awareness of articulation are required for this piece. Make sure that the triplets don't sound like two semiquavers and a quaver! It may be helpful to think of bars 1-6 in a taut $\frac{4}{4}$, then bars 7-16 in a flowing $\frac{2}{2}$.

17. Rangefinder

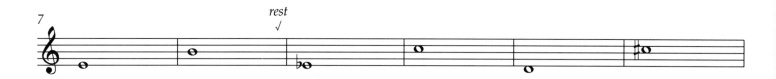

Play each note separately, keeping the pitch even throughout. As an alternative, count four quavers *crescendo* and four quavers *diminuendo* on each note. This is very demanding, so rest well afterwards. At a more advanced level, play the study a tone higher, and extend it by six bars thus:

18. The Fourth

For this study, try to find a feel which encompasses both driving semiquavers, and more relaxed, flowing quavers. All phrases begin with the same note, bottom E. Study the trumpet sonata by Paul Hindemith, which uses the interval of a fourth as an integral part of the melodic and harmonic structure.

19. Easy Does It

In working towards the high register, concentrate on building the central embouchure muscles gradually and without strain. Therefore easy does it but practise **regularly**. This exercise is made more useful by transposition: down a tone to G for preparation, and up to B♭ and C when A major has become really fluent.

20. Major-Minor Arpeggios

At the slow tempo concentrate on floating the sound equally over the whole range. To do this imagine a slight *crescendo* when going up. Remember that increased air flow is required for each higher note. Towards the upper speed develop flexibility of embouchure. Work from a fairly comfortable dynamic level towards a well controlled *pianissimo*. This can also be practised articulated: (1) two slurred, two tongued, (2) all tongued, (3) staccato, and (4) marcato and sostenuto for endurance.

21. Seventh Heaven

The symphonies of Gustav Mahler, and many of the second Viennese school works, abound in wide lyrical slurs. Here aim for an even, sweet sound. This definitely requires much support of the airstream plus use of the embouchure in the upward jumps. Remember also that even very slow music requires firm fingers.

22. Alpine Waltz

Jaunty ♩=148

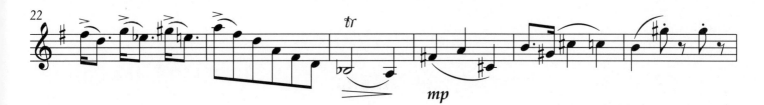

This slightly cheeky waltz needs a good, firm sense of rhythm, with some weight on every downbeat. Take care to play trills elegantly – but not too fast. I suggest the following interpretation:

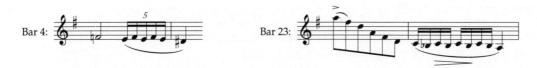

23. Minor Ninths and Rhythm

Fathom the rhythmic complexities of this piece by practising slowly with a metronome.

24. Vienna

This exercise has the flavour of a symphony written in Vienna in 1904. The work has a prominent trumpet part. Can you identify it?

25. Computer Failure

This study is daunting at first sight, but consists mainly of simple major triads. With practice it will help develop good co-ordination of firm fingers and steady rhythm. At optimum speed, triple tongueing will be essential.

26. Thirds

The character of this study is that of a good-natured romp, so try to avoid any hint of hardness. Think of a bouncing crotchet beat in the first section, and add a touch of *crescendo* in bars 3, 5 etc. By contrast, the trio may be smoothly phrased.

27. Rhythmic Rondo

Skipping ♩=136

Here, many of the rhythms look more difficult than they are in practice. Count quavers in bar 2 to set up bar 3. The syncopated but regular rhythm in bar 19 merely continues in bar 20, and the accents in bar 20 set up the dotted crotchet pulse in bar 21. Similarly the accents in bars 29-31 set up the pulse in bar 32.

28. Greased Lightning

Works such as Rimsky-Korsakov's *Sheherazade* and Ravel's orchestration of Musorgsky's *Pictures* demand great skill of articulation along with considerable stamina. Therefore, try to develop both qualities in parallel, aiming for consistency and clarity throughout the study.

29. Perpetuum Mobile

Accented and rhythmic ♪=240

Here, both rhythm and pitch structures are compound. $\frac{11}{16}$ is subdivided into units of two, three and four, and speed can be increased gradually until the rhythm sounds natural. Triads have been extended to arpeggios of the thirteenth, some in wholetones. Look at the ballerina's dance in Stravinsky's *Petrushka* or the H. W. Henze *Sonatina* for solo trumpet.

30. Mr Logic

The first eight bars of this piece emphasise the interval of an augmented fourth, and include all twelve chromatic pitches in a jumbled order. See if you can similarly decypher the logical structure of the entire piece. Look at Peter Maxwell Davies' *Sonata* for trumpet and piano.

TRUMPET VOLUMES

from Faber Music

Improve your sight-reading! Grades 1–5 *Paul Harris & John Davies* ISBN 0-571-50989-4

Improve your sight-reading! Grades 5–8 *Paul Harris & John Davies* ISBN 0-571-51152-X

Jazz with the Greats *Chris Goddard* ISBN 0-571-51279-8

Progressive Studies *John Miller* ISBN 0-571-51320-4

Simple Studies for Beginner Brass *John Miller* ISBN 0-571-50934-7

Trumpet Basics (pupil's book) *John Miller* ISBN 0-571-51998-9

Trumpet Basics (teacher's book) *John Miller* ISBN 0-571-51997-0

Progressive Jazz Studies *James Rae* ISBN 0-571-51543-6

The Baroque Trumpet *edited by John Miller* ISBN 0-571-51704-8

First Book of Trumpet Solos *edited by John Miller & John Wallace* ISBN 0-571-50846-4

Second Book of Trumpet Solos *edited by John Miller & John Wallace* ISBN 0-571-50857-X

Going Solo *arranged by John Miller & Leslie Pearson* ISBN 0-571-51425-1

Play Ballads *arranged by John Kember* ISBN 0-571-51996-2

The Victorian Trumpet *edited by John Wallace & Tony Rickard* ISBN 0-571-52053-7

Unbeaten Tracks for trumpet and piano *edited by John Miller* ISBN 0-571-52005-7

Play Jazztime *arranged by Robert Farley* ISBN 0-571-52045-6

Play Latin *arranged by Robert Farley* ISBN 0-571-52046-4

Up-Grade! Trumpet Grades 1–2 *Pam Wedgwood* ISBN 0-571-52131-2

Up-Grade! Trumpet Grades 2–3 *Pam Wedgwood* ISBN 0-571-52122-3

FABER *ff* MUSIC